D1071875

PRESIDENTS

THEODORE ROOSEVELT

A MyReportLinks.com Book

Donald G. Schueler

MyReportLinks.com Books

an imprint of

Enslow Publishers, Inc.

Box 398, 40 Industrial Road
Berkeley Heights, NJ 07922
USA

MyReportLinks.com Books, an imprint of Enslow Publishers, Inc.

Library of Congress Cataloging-in-Publication Data

Schueler, Donald G.
  Theodore Roosevelt / Donald G. Schueler.
     p. cm. — (Presidents)
Summary: Traces the life of the man who has been called our nation's
first modern president.
  ISBN 0-7660-5008-4
  1. Roosevelt, Theodore, 1858–1919—Juvenile literature. 2.
Presidents—United States—Biography—Juvenile literature. [1.
Roosevelt, Theodore, 1858–1919. 2. Presidents.] I. Title. II. Series.
  E757 .S37 2002
  973.91'1'092—dc21
  [B]
                                        2001004270

Printed in the United States of America

10 9 8 7 6 5 4 3 2 1

To Our Readers:
Through the purchase of this book, you and your library gain access to the Report Links that specifically back up this book.
The Publisher will provide access to the Report Links that back up this book and will keep these Report Links up to date on **www.myreportlinks.com** for three years from the book's first publication date.
We have done our best to make sure all Internet addresses in this book were active and appropriate when we went to press. However, the author and the Publisher have no control over, and assume no liability for, the material available on those Internet sites or on other Web sites they may link to.
The usage of the MyReportLinks.com Books Web site is subject to the terms and conditions stated on the Usage Policy Statement on **www.myreportlinks.com**.
In the future, a password may be required to access the Report Links that back up this book. The password is found on the bottom of page 4 of this book.
Any comments or suggestions can be sent by e-mail to comments@myreportlinks.com or to the address on the back cover.

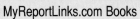
Contents

MyReportLinks.com Books
Great Books, Great Links, Great for Research!

MyReportLinks.com Books present the information you need to learn about your report subject. In addition, they show you where to go on the Internet for more information. The pre-evaluated Report Links that back up this book are kept up to date on **www.myreportlinks.com**. With the purchase of a MyReportLinks.com Books title, you and your library gain access to the Report Links that specifically back up that book. The Report Links save hours of research time and link to dozens—even hundreds—of Web sites, source documents, and photos related to your report topic.

Please see "To Our Readers" on the Copyright page for important information about this book, the MyReportLinks.com Books Web site, and the Report Links that back up this book.

Access:

The Publisher will provide access to the Report Links that back up this book and will try to keep these Report Links up to date on our Web site for three years from the book's first publication date. Please enter **PRS125F** if asked for a password.

The Internet sites described below can be accessed at
http://www.myreportlinks.com

*EDITOR'S CHOICE

▶**Theodore Roosevelt Association**
The Theodore Roosevelt Association Web site offers a wealth of
information about T.R., including a time line, biography, presidential
facts, film clips, and a section on Roosevelt's unprecedented
contributions to conservation.

Link to this Internet site from http://www.myreportlinks.com

*EDITOR'S CHOICE

▶**Theodore Roosevelt,
26th President of the United States**
This site provides facts and figures on Theodore Roosevelt, with links
to election results, cabinet members, historical documents, and
media resources.

Link to this Internet site from http://www.myreportlinks.com

*EDITOR'S CHOICE

▶**Theodore Roosevelt**
The American Experience series provides a comprehensive look at
Theodore Roosevelt, including his early career, presidential politics,
domestic policy, foreign affairs, and legacy.

Link to this Internet site from http://www.myreportlinks.com

*EDITOR'S CHOICE

▶**T.R.: Theodore Roosevelt, 26th President of the
United States of America**
This site offers an assortment of information about Theodore
Roosevelt, including photographs, films, speeches, and books written
by Roosevelt.

Link to this Internet site from http://www.myreportlinks.com

*EDITOR'S CHOICE

▶**Theodore Roosevelt: Icon of the American Century**
At this site you can take a virtual tour through the life of Theodore
Roosevelt. Learn about his experiences as a hunter and his achievements
as president.

Link to this Internet site from http://www.myreportlinks.com

*EDITOR'S CHOICE

▶**Theodore Roosevelt and His Quest for Glory**
This four-part essay examines the controversy surrounding Roosevelt's
quest for the Medal of Honor. Theodore Roosevelt was posthumously
awarded the medal in 2001, by President Clinton, who cited
Roosevelt's bravery in battle during the Spanish-American War.

Link to this Internet site from http://www.myreportlinks.com

Report Links

The Internet sites described below can be accessed at
http://www.myreportlinks.com

▶**The American President: Expanding Power**
This PBS site is dedicated to presidents who have expanded the chief executive's power. Here you will find a brief description of Roosevelt, a historical document, and a video clip.

Link to this Internet site from http://www.myreportlinks.com

▶**American Presidents: Theodore Roosevelt**
This site contains "Life Facts" and "Did you know?" trivia about Theodore Roosevelt. You will also find a letter written by Roosevelt and links to his birthplace and grave site.

Link to this Internet site from http://www.myreportlinks.com

▶**The Emergence of Modern America (1890–1930)**
Upton Sinclair's novel *The Jungle* prompted Theodore Roosevelt to support the Meat Inspection Act of 1907. At this site you will find a portion of a letter written by Sinclair to Roosevelt.

Link to this Internet site from http://www.myreportlinks.com

▶**The Indomitable President**
This site provides a comprehensive biography of Theodore Roosevelt. You will also find links to his domestic and foreign policy, family life, and his legacy.

Link to this Internet site from http://www.myreportlinks.com

▶**Lt. Quentin Roosevelt**
At this Web site you will find a brief biography of Theodore Roosevelt's youngest son, Quentin. Here you will learn about his military career and his legacy as a war hero.

Link to this Internet site from http://www.myreportlinks.com

▶**Meet Amazing Americans: Theodore Roosevelt**
America's Story from America's Library, a Library of Congress Web site, provides a brief introduction to Theodore Roosevelt. Here you will learn about the Rough Riders, Roosevelt's affection for animals, and his connection to the teddy bear.

Link to this Internet site from http://www.myreportlinks.com

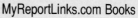
Report Links

The Internet sites described below can be accessed at
http://www.myreportlinks.com

▶**Nobel e-Museum: Theodore Roosevelt**
In 1906, Theodore Roosevelt was awarded the Nobel Peace Prize for
negotiating an end to the Russo-Japanese War. At this site you will find
the presentation speech, Roosevelt's Nobel lecture, and a profile of
his life.

Link to this Internet site from http://www.myreportlinks.com

▶**Objects from the Presidency**
At this site you will find objects related to President Theodore
Roosevelt and a description of the era he lived in. You will also learn
about the office of the presidency.

Link to this Internet site from http://www.myreportlinks.com

▶**On This Day**
This article from the *New York Times* provides a history of the Russo-
Japanese War and discusses how Theodore Roosevelt became a central
figure in resolving the conflict.

Link to this Internet site from http://www.myreportlinks.com

▶**Russo-Japanese War**
This site provides a brief history of the Russo-Japanese War. Here you
will learn how Roosevelt brought an end to the war.

Link to this Internet site from http://www.myreportlinks.com

▶**Teddy Roosevelt**
At this Web site you will find an overview of Theodore Roosevelt's life
and a list of his numerous accomplishments.

Link to this Internet site from http://www.myreportlinks.com

▶**Teddy Roosevelt and the Rough Riders: July 1, 1898**
America's Story from America's Library, a Library of Congress Web site,
provides a brief history of Roosevelt and the formation of the
Rough Riders.

Link to this Internet site from http://www.myreportlinks.com

Report Links

The Internet sites described below can be accessed at
http://www.myreportlinks.com

▶**Theodore Roosevelt**
Here you will find a biography of Theodore Roosevelt, links to his inaugural address, and quick facts about his life.

Link to this Internet site from http://www.myreportlinks.com

▶**Theodore Roosevelt**
Here you will find a collection of books, essays, and letters written by Theodore Roosevelt. You will also find quotations and writings about Roosevelt.

Link to this Internet site from http://www.myreportlinks.com

▶**Theodore Roosevelt (1858–1919)**
The Smithsonian Archive of American Art holds a collection of art related to Theodore Roosevelt. Included are a letter, cartoons, postcards, and photographs from various artists.

Link to this Internet site from http://www.myreportlinks.com

▶**Theodore Roosevelt: Bully for North Dakota!**
At this site you will learn about Theodore Roosevelt's experiences in North Dakota. You can also explore Theodore Roosevelt National Park in the Badlands.

Link to this Internet site from http://www.myreportlinks.com

▶**Theodore Roosevelt: Conservation as the Guardian of Democracy**
At this site you will find an essay that explores Theodore Roosevelt's commitment to conservation.

Link to this Internet site from http://www.myreportlinks.com

▶**Theodore Roosevelt Papers at the Library of Congress**
At this site you will find an essay that explores Theodore Roosevelt the historian and explains how the Library of Congress acquired his papers. You will also find entries from Roosevelt's diary and photographs.

Link to this Internet site from http://www.myreportlinks.com

Report Links

> The Internet sites described below can be accessed at
> **http://www.myreportlinks.com**

▶**TR, The Story of Theodore Roosevelt**
At this site you will find an interview and a time line of events that
occurred during Roosevelt's administration. You will also learn about
his legacy.

Link to this Internet site from http://www.myreportlinks.com

▶**The White House: Edith Kermit Carow Roosevelt**
The official White House Web site holds the biography of Edith
Kermit Carow Roosevelt. Here you will learn that Edith and Theodore
Roosevelt were longtime companions.

Link to this Internet site from http://www.myreportlinks.com

▶**The White House: Theodore Roosevelt**
The official White House Web site holds the biography of Theodore
Roosevelt. Here you will learn about the accomplishments of the
youngest man to serve as a United States president.

Link to this Internet site from http://www.myreportlinks.com

▶**William Howard Taft: The Reluctant President**
This Web site provides a comprehensive biography of William Howard
Taft, who succeeded Theodore Roosevelt as president. Taft's admiration
for Roosevelt and his desire to carry on the former president's agenda
are explained.

Link to this Internet site from http://www.myreportlinks.com

▶**The World of 1898: The Spanish-American War**
By navigating through this site you will find an introduction to the
Spanish-American War, links to a brief biography of Theodore
Roosevelt, and an essay about the war.

Link to this Internet site from http://www.myreportlinks.com

▶**1904: Alton Parker vs. Theodore Roosevelt**
At this site you will find a brief summary of Roosevelt's public career
and the election of 1904. You can also read an excerpt from the *New
York Times* about Roosevelt's victory in the election.

Link to this Internet site from http://www.myreportlinks.com

Highlights

1858—*Oct. 27:* Theodore "Teddy" Roosevelt is born in New York City.

1878—His father, Theodore Roosevelt, Sr., dies.

1880—Graduates from Harvard College.

—*Oct. 27:* Marries Alice Hathaway Lee.

1881—Elected to New York State Assembly. Serves three one-year terms.

1884—*Feb. 14:* Teddy's mother, Martha Bulloch Roosevelt, dies, followed eleven hours later by his wife, Alice.

1886—*Dec 2:* Marries Edith Kermit Carow.

1889–1898—Holds various appointed positions in government, including U.S. Civil Service Commissioner.

1898—*May–September:* Serves with First U.S. Volunteer Cavalry Regiment in the Spanish-American War.

—*July 1:* Leads charges up Kettle Hill and San Juan Hill in the Battle of San Juan Heights with his Rough Riders.

—*Nov. 8:* Elected governor of New York.

1900—William McKinley reelected president; Roosevelt, his running mate, is vice president.

1901—*Sept. 6:* President McKinley is shot, and dies on September 14. Roosevelt becomes president.

1904—Runs for president and is elected by a large majority.

1905—Establishes the U.S. Forest Service, now part of the Department of Agriculture.

1906—Wins Nobel Peace Prize for negotiating an end to the Russo-Japanese War.

1912—Creates Progressive Party and runs as third-party candidate for president.

1912—Survives assassination attempt.

1919—*Jan. 6:* Dies at sixty years of age, at home on Long Island.

2001—*Jan. 16:* Theodore Roosevelt posthumously awarded the Congressional Medal of Honor for "conspicuous gallantry in action" during his service in the Spanish-American War.

The Great Day

It was July 1, 1898. A war between Spain and the United States was under way. Cuba was the battleground. The Spanish army was entrenched atop a series of hills called the San Juan Heights, which overlooked the city of Santiago. At the bottom of the slope, American soldiers were pinned down, raked by Spanish gunfire and exploding shells.

This was how matters stood when Colonel Theodore Roosevelt arrived on the scene with his volunteer regiment. They were an oddball collection of cowboys, college athletes, American Indians, and New York policemen. Although the press had nicknamed them the "Rough Riders," Roosevelt was the only one on a horse.

All at once the colonel led his men in a charge up the slope. He rode through the regular army troops at the bottom of the hill. He galloped back and forth in front of the lines. Bullets whistled and shells burst all around him. Roosevelt challenged the regulars to follow the example of his volunteers. When one soldier hesitated, Roosevelt angrily yelled, "Are you afraid to stand up when I am on horseback?"[1] Shamed, the man did stand up and was instantly killed by a Spanish bullet. Roosevelt was nicked in the arm, but nothing could stop him. He inspired the men. They suffered heavy casualties in this heroic charge, but they won the hill. Roosevelt was one of the first to reach the top. The battle that took place in the San Juan

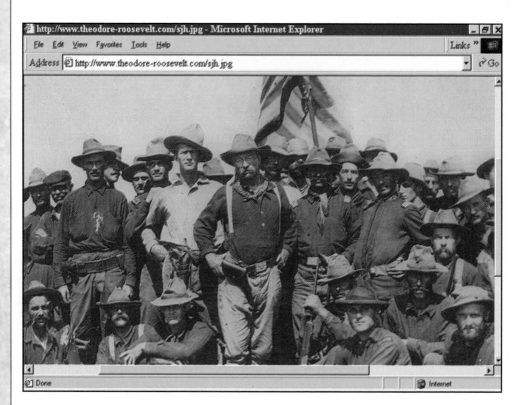

http://www.theodore-roosevelt.com/sjh.jpg - Microsoft Internet Explorer

File   Edit   View   Favorites   Tools   Help   Links »

Address http://www.theodore-roosevelt.com/sjh.jpg   Go

Done   Internet

▲ *Surrounded by his Rough Riders, Colonel Theodore Roosevelt is pictured after the Battle of San Juan Heights. Roosevelt described the victorious charges he led on July 1, 1898, at San Juan as "the great day of my life."*

Heights that day proved to be the most decisive victory on land in the Spanish-American War.

Roosevelt had lived for just such a day all his life. He had always wanted to be a hero. Now he had proved he was one. He had also proved that he could take decisive action and that he was a natural leader whom other men would follow. Many years later, not long before he died, he still concluded, "San Juan was the great day of my life."[2]

Chapter 2 ▶

Weakness Into Strength, 1858–1880

When Theodore Roosevelt was a child, no one would have guessed that he would become one of the most forceful and physically vigorous presidents ever to occupy the White House. He was a sickly little boy who suffered from headaches, fevers, and asthma.

▶ Early Life

Theodore "Teddy" Roosevelt was born on October 27, 1858, in New York City. He was the second of four children. His sister Anna was the eldest; his brother Elliot and sister Corinne were younger. His parents were very loving and very well-off. His father, Theodore Roosevelt, Sr., came from a family that had made a fortune selling imported glass and buying real estate.

His mother, Martha Bulloch Roosevelt, was from Georgia. Three years after Teedie was born ("Teedie" was what he preferred to be called as a child by his family and friends), the Civil War started. All his mother's relatives fought on the Confederate side. Teedie's father wanted to fight for the Union, but Martha persuaded him to hire a substitute, which was allowed in those days. She could not bear the thought of her husband fighting against her brothers and cousins. In later years, Theodore, Sr., was a little ashamed that he had not enlisted.[1] Teedie may have wished his father had served in the war as well.[2] He made a youthful resolution that if ever there were another war, he would jump at the chance to fight for his country.

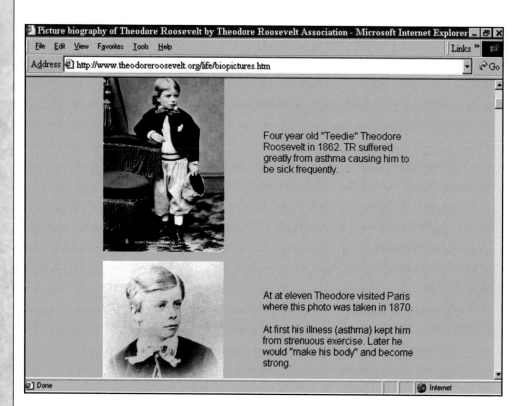

Picture biography of Theodore Roosevelt by Theodore Roosevelt Association - Microsoft Internet Explorer

File   Edit   View   Favorites   Tools   Help   Links »

Address http://www.theodoreroosevelt.org/life/biopictures.htm   Go

Four year old "Teedie" Theodore Roosevelt in 1862. TR suffered greatly from asthma causing him to be sick frequently.

At at eleven Theodore visited Paris where this photo was taken in 1870.

At first his illness (asthma) kept him from strenuous exercise. Later he would "make his body" and become strong.

Done   Internet

These photographs of Theodore Roosevelt as a child show him at age four and age eleven. Often ill, Teedie (as he liked to be called) worked hard during his early teens to overcome his frail health by following a rigorous exercise program.

▶ A Father's Influence

Teedie might have felt badly that his father did not fight in the Civil War, but he loved and admired him more than anyone else in the world. Theodore, Sr., was renowned for donating money to charities. But much more important from Teedie's point of view, his father was the one who carried him about the house in the night hours when he suffered terrible asthma attacks. And it was his father who encouraged him to believe that he did not have to be sick and puny all his life. He said that with the help of willpower and a lot of exercise, Teedie could make his body strong.[3]

Recipe for a "Strenuous Life"

Teedie took the lesson to heart. By his early teens he was lifting weights, wrestling, swimming, and hiking. He developed a love for the outdoors and for nature study. He liked to hunt and brought home many a luckless bird or small animal that he stuffed and added to his rather smelly collection of specimens.

Teedie became a great believer in the "strenuous life."[4] But partly because he was sometimes too sick to play outside, partly because of his father's example, he also loved to read. When he was eleven, he was finally fitted with glasses that corrected his poor eyesight. After that he gobbled up one book after another. He especially liked adventure tales like *The Saga of King Olaf,* found in a Longfellow poem, and the *Nibelungenlied,* a German epic poem that featured heroes who were noble and brave.[5]

Education

Because he was often sick as a child, Teedie never saw the inside of a school until he went to college. He did get a good education, though. His father encouraged his interest in history, geography, and natural history. And he learned about foreign countries when he traveled with his family to Europe and more distant places like Egypt.

In 1875, when Teedie was eighteen, he entered Harvard College, in Cambridge, Massachusetts. It was the first time in his life that he had been away from his family. At first he had a hard time fitting in. Some of his classmates felt he was a little weird because he was such a fanatic

about physical exercise and because he kept snakes and lizards in his room. And even by the strict moral standards of the time, he had strong views of right and wrong. He felt he should never do anything he would be ashamed to admit to his father or anyone else. He did not smoke, and he did not drink much. He taught Sunday school at an Episcopal church. And he made no secret of disapproving of men and women who had sex before they married.

▶ Facing Challenges

With his usual determination, however, he made a great success of his later years at Harvard. His efforts to strengthen his sickly body began to pay off. His asthma improved. And during a summer hunting trip in the Maine wilderness, he proved that he could handle any physical challenge by keeping up with his tough woodsman guide while living off the land for weeks on end.

He faced another kind of challenge when his father, whom Roosevelt called "the best man I ever knew,"[6] died of cancer early in 1878. Theodore Roosevelt was heartbroken, but he resolved to carry on as his father would have wished. He was more self-confident now that he was on his own. He studied hard and got good grades. He made many new friends. And because his father had left him a lot of money in his will, Roosevelt was a rich young man. He was able to throw parties, buy fine clothes, and have his own horse and buggy.

The most exciting challenge of all, though, was winning the heart of Alice Hathaway Lee. Alice was the cousin of a Harvard classmate. They had met at a weekend party. Roosevelt fell madly in love with her and courted her during his junior and senior years at Harvard. At first she put him off, but finally she agreed to be his wife. He wrote,

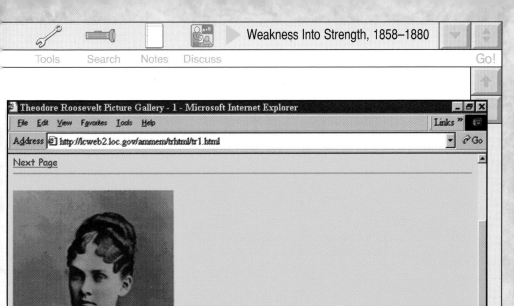

Alice Hathaway Lee Roosevelt (1st wife of President Theodore Roosevelt)

Prints and Photographs Division, Library of Congress. *Reproduction #:LC-USZ62-25802*

Theodore Roosevelt courted Alice Hathaway Lee, the cousin of one of his college classmates, during his last two years at Harvard. They were married on October 27, 1880—which also happened to be Roosevelt's twenty-second birthday.

"How she, so pure and sweet and beautiful, can think of marrying me I can not understand, but I praise and thank God it is so."[7] They were married on October 27, 1880, his twenty-second birthday.

"Challenge" is a key word in trying to understand what made Theodore Roosevelt tick. By the time he graduated from college, he had transformed himself from a shy, sickly youth into a strong, energetic man whom others admired. He had set himself a test, and he had passed it. He would go on testing himself, and others, for the rest of his life.

Chapter 3

Getting Ahead, 1880–1901

Like many other young people, Theodore Roosevelt was not sure what he wanted to do in life. He only knew that he wanted to do something important with his life. He studied law, but it did not interest him very much. He published *The Naval History of the War of 1812*, but he was too outgoing to enjoy the lonely work of being a writer. He began to dabble in state politics in his native New York. In his day, even more than now, the Democratic and Republican parties were run by "party machines" at the state and local levels. Roosevelt did not object to political parties being organized. However, corruption was the rule in the party machines. Through what was called the "spoils system," party bosses made themselves rich and paid off their supporters with public funds.

Roosevelt joined New York City's Republican Party. The party supported him when he ran for state representative in 1881 because they thought he would appeal to upper-class voters in his district. He won, and in 1882 he became a member of the state legislature. But in contrast to what the party machine wanted, he fought against the spoils system and soon earned a reputation as a reformer.

▶ Tragedy Strikes

On February 14, 1884, Theodore Roosevelt suffered two great losses. First, his mother died of typhoid fever. Then a few hours later, upstairs in the same house, his wife, Alice, died of Bright's disease. Just two days earlier she had given

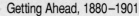

birth to a healthy baby girl. Deeply depressed, he wrote, "For joy or for sorrow my life has now been lived out."[1] He would not talk to anyone about Alice. Instead, he left his daughter, also named Alice, in the care of his sister Anna, and he buried himself in his work as a legislator.

Later in 1884, Roosevelt opposed the nomination of James C. Blaine as the Republican Party's presidential candidate because he believed Blaine was corrupt. Blaine won the nomination anyway. An angry Roosevelt was tempted to leave the Republican Party. In the end, though, he

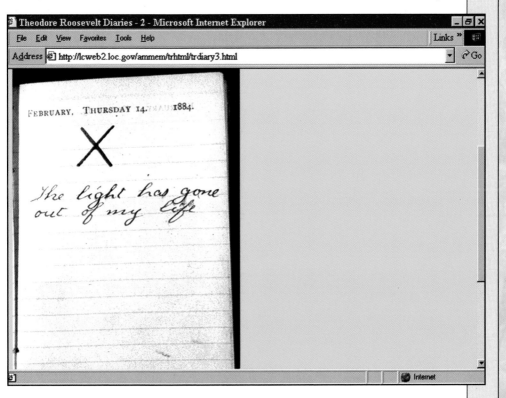

▲ On one tragic day, February 14, 1884, Theodore Roosevelt lost his mother and then his wife. His wife had given birth only two days earlier to their daughter. This diary entry from February 14 speaks of the heartbreak that Theodore Roosevelt must have felt that day.

decided to support Blaine. Roosevelt fought all his life for honest government, but he was learning that in politics, compromise was often necessary.

Blaine lost the general election to the Democratic candidate, Grover Cleveland. Roosevelt, still grieving for his wife, decided not to serve another term in the New York legislature. He headed west to the Dakota Territory, where he had bought a cattle ranch a year earlier.

▶ Life as a Cowboy

Roosevelt admired the cowboys he worked with for the same reason that he admired the men he had hunted with in Maine. They were "self-reliant," he wrote, because "their life forces them to be both daring and adventurous."[2] Roosevelt felt that was the way he must live, too. Even though he was an Easterner who had a squeaky voice and wore glasses, the cowboys and ranchers he came to know respected him. He organized a stockmen's association that made rules about grazing rights for the association's members. The purpose of such rules was to keep the range from being overgrazed. When he realized that the grizzly bears and other wildlife he hunted were becoming scarce, he started the Boone and Crockett Club. The club's goal was to preserve big-game species. These experiences influenced Roosevelt's later efforts as president to preserve the nation's wildlife and other natural resources.

Roosevelt loved the West, but he realized he would never get ahead in politics if he stayed there. He moved back East, and in December 1886, he remarried. His second wife, Edith Carow, had been a friend since childhood. She loved Theodore Roosevelt and shared many of his enthusiasms, but she did not see herself living in a log cabin on the prairie. During the terrible winter of

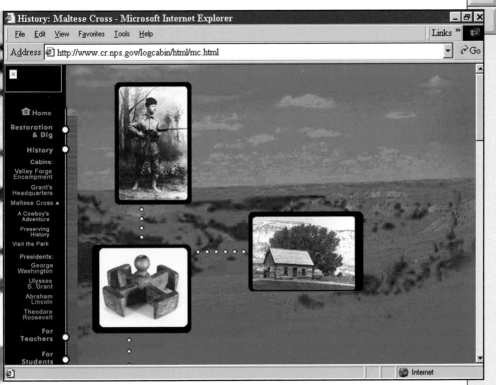

History: Maltese Cross - Microsoft Internet Explorer

File   Edit   View   Favorites   Tools   Help   Links »

Address http://www.cr.nps.gov/logcabin/html/mc.html   Go

Home
Restoration & Dig
History
Cabins:
Valley Forge Encampment
Grant's Headquarters
Maltese Cross •
A Cowboy's Adventure
Preserving History
Visit the Park
Presidents:
George Washington
Ulysses S. Grant
Abraham Lincoln
Theodore Roosevelt
For Teachers
For Students

Internet

▲ *Following the deaths of his mother and his wife, Roosevelt headed west, to the Dakota Territory, where he purchased a ranch and lived among men who were both much poorer and hardier than he was. The ranch became known by its brand, the Maltese Cross. Roosevelt's experiences in the American West led him to the realization that the wilderness of the United States needed to be preserved and protected.*

1886–87, most of Roosevelt's cattle froze to death. He lost his ranch and much of his fortune.

▶ Return to Politics

Roosevelt ran for mayor of New York City in 1886 and was soundly defeated. During the next twelve years, he managed to stay in politics by holding appointed positions in government. President Benjamin Harrison appointed him to the Civil Service Commission in 1888. Under

Roosevelt's guidance the commission saw to it that federal employees got their jobs on the basis of merit, not because some politician owed them a favor. He was reappointed to the commission by President Grover Cleveland in 1893. Since he was living in Washington, D.C., he got to know many important people who would help him later on.

In 1894, Roosevelt was offered a chance to run for mayor of New York City again. Edith did not want to leave Washington and convinced him to refuse. This was not the only time he took his wife's advice. Throughout his life, she often balanced his rashness with a calm level-headedness.[3] However, by 1895, the Roosevelts moved back to New York because Roosevelt was appointed to the board of the New York City Police Commission and became its president. For two years he tried to clean up the police department. He became famous for walking the streets late at night, surprising policemen who were taking payoffs or sleeping on the job.

When William McKinley, a Republican, became president in 1896, he brought Roosevelt back to Washington as the assistant secretary of the navy. Roosevelt enjoyed his work, especially since the secretary of the navy, John Long, was often ill and left him in charge. Roosevelt believed in the importance of a strong navy and did much to increase its strength. He loved the idea of a good fight, and he argued that America should be ready and willing to go to war to protect its economic or military interests anywhere in the world. He especially felt that the Western Hemisphere should be free of foreign influence. Roosevelt also supported United States control of Hawaii, the Philippines, and Cuba for strategic purposes.

Tools   Search   Notes   Discuss   Go!

Almanac of Theodore Roosevelt Family - Microsoft Internet Explorer

File Edit View Favorites Tools Help   Links »

Address   http://www.theodore-roosevelt.com/trfamily.html   Go

I tell you, Kermit, it was great comfort to feel, all during the last days when affairs looked doubtful, that no matter how things came out the really important thing was the lovely life I have with Mother and with you children, and that compared to this home life everything else was of very small importance from the standpoint of happiness.

- Theodore Roosevelt

Done   Internet

▲ Roosevelt's second marriage, in 1886, was to a woman who had been his friend since childhood—Edith Carow. The Roosevelt family eventually numbered six children in all, and Theodore Roosevelt found great happiness and comfort in his sons and daughters. His youngest son, Quentin, is missing from this photograph.

▶ Spanish-American War

In 1897, Cuba was a colony of Spain. The Cuban peasants had revolted against Spanish rule and were demanding independence. Roosevelt and many others saw this uprising as a good excuse for getting rid of an unpopular foreign power that was too close to American shores. At first, President McKinley was unwilling to involve the United States. Then an incident happened that forced him to act. An American warship, the USS *Maine*, had been sent to Cuba to protect American citizens from the rioting that

was going on there. A few days after it arrived at the port of Havana, in February of 1898, the *Maine* was blown up in a huge explosion. More than 250 American sailors were killed. The explosion was blamed on sabotage by Spain (though naval experts now think a malfunction of the ship's boilers was the cause of the explosion). The American public demanded war with Spain. McKinley gave in, and Congress declared war on Spain on April 25, a day after Spain declared war on the United States.

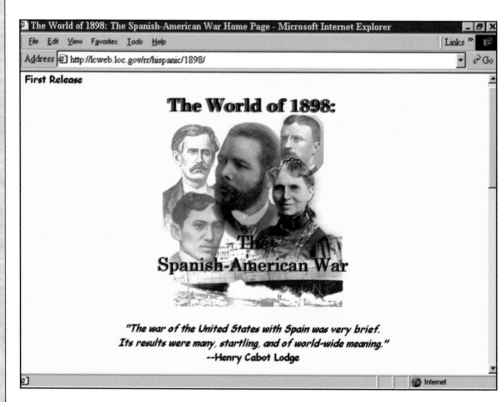

▲ When the United States declared war on Spain, on April 25, 1898, Theodore Roosevelt was elated because he saw it as an opportunity to finally test himself in battle. He resigned his position as assistant secretary of the navy and volunteered for a cavalry regiment. His brief but glorious service in the Spanish-American War made him a national hero.

Roosevelt was overjoyed. He wanted to see the United States flex its muscles as a world power, and he now had a chance to prove himself in battle. He resigned as assistant secretary of the navy and volunteered as a lieutenant colonel in the First U.S. Volunteer Cavalry Regiment.

By this time, Theodore and Edith Roosevelt had six children. There were two daughters—Alice, from Roosevelt's first marriage, and Ethel, from his second— and four sons—Theodore, Kermit, Archibald, and Quentin. When Theodore Roosevelt was about to enlist, Edith had just given birth to Quentin and was still recovering from a serious operation. As greatly as Roosevelt loved his wife and family, it was typical of him that he did not let anything stop him from going off to war. He arrived in Cuba with his regiment, which came to be known as the Rough Riders, in June 1898.

On June 30, the eve of what was to be his greatest battle, Roosevelt was promoted by his commanding officer, Major General Leonard Wood, to colonel. The next day, July 1, Roosevelt led his Rough Riders in valiant charges up Kettle Hill and San Juan Hill. The courage he displayed in those battles was later matched by his commitment to save his troops after the fighting had ceased. More American servicemen in Cuba were dying from malaria and other illnesses than had died in battle. Roosevelt and others pressed the army to have the Rough Riders and other troops that were still stationed in Cuba sent home.

▶ A Kick Upstairs

After the war, Roosevelt returned home a national hero. His popularity led the party bosses to nominate him as the Republican candidate for governor of New York in 1898. Even so, they worried about whether they could control

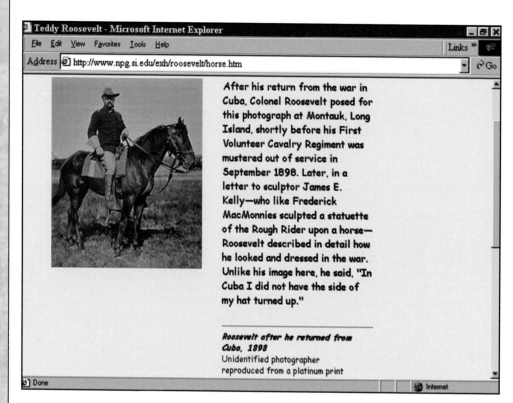

After his return from the war in Cuba, Colonel Roosevelt posed for this photograph at Montauk, Long Island, shortly before his First Volunteer Cavalry Regiment was mustered out of service in September 1898. Later, in a letter to sculptor James E. Kelly—who like Frederick MacMonnies sculpted a statuette of the Rough Rider upon a horse—Roosevelt described in detail how he looked and dressed in the war. Unlike his image here, he said, "In Cuba I did not have the side of my hat turned up."

Roosevelt after he returned from Cuba, 1898
Unidentified photographer
reproduced from a platinum print

▲ Even after the fighting in Cuba ended, American troops continued to suffer and die from malaria and other diseases. Angered by bureaucratic delays, Theodore Roosevelt was instrumental in pressing the U.S. Army to have the Rough Riders sent home in August of 1898.

him if he won. When he did win, they found out that on some important issues they could not. Over their objections, he supported a bill that made some companies pay a tax for the right to have monopolies on (complete control over) services such as railroads and streetcar lines. He also sometimes refused to appoint the people the bosses recommended for important government jobs.

In those days, New York governors were elected for two-year terms. By the time Roosevelt's first term was coming to an end, the party machine in New York was eager to get rid of him. They decided that the best way to do this was to "kick him upstairs"—in other words, get him out of state politics.

In 1900, McKinley was running for a second term as president. The man who had been his vice president during his first term, Garret Hobart, had died. The New York bosses proposed Roosevelt as the replacement. At first, Roosevelt was reluctant. The vice presidency was thought of as a do-nothing job. He agreed to take the nomination only when he realized that he might not win another term as governor without the support of the party machine. Once he did accept the nomination, he campaigned hard for McKinley and the Republican platform. Never one to mince words, Roosevelt accused the Democrats of being hypocrites and traitors. McKinley and Roosevelt won by a large majority.

Roosevelt would not be vice president for long, however. On September 6, 1901, only six months after being reelected, President McKinley was shot at the Pan-American Exposition, in Buffalo, New York. He died eight days later. Suddenly, unexpectedly, Roosevelt was president of the United States. It bothered him that he had not been elected to the office, but from the first, he loved being president. He soon realized it was the best position in the world to be in if you wanted people to listen to you.

Chapter 4

A New Sort of President, 1901–1909

Theodore Roosevelt was sworn in as president on September 14, 1901, in Buffalo, New York, by U.S. District Court Judge John R. Hazel. At forty-two years of age, Roosevelt was the youngest man ever to become

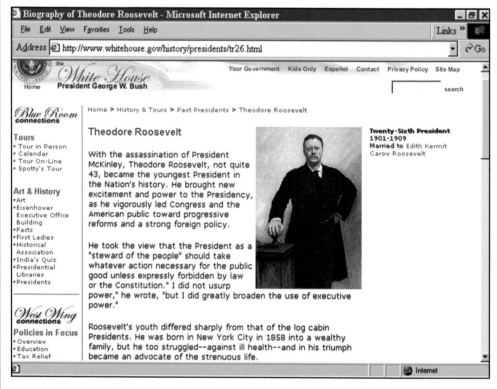

Biography of Theodore Roosevelt - Microsoft Internet Explorer

File   Edit   View   Favorites   Tools   Help   Links ”

Address http://www.whitehouse.gov/history/presidents/tr26.html   Go

the White House
President George W. Bush

Your Government   Kids Only   Español   Contact   Privacy Policy   Site Map

search

Home > History & Tours > Past Presidents > Theodore Roosevelt

Blue Room connections

Tours
* Tour in Person
* Calendar
* Tour On-Line
* Spotty's Tour

Art & History
* Art
* Eisenhower Executive Office Building
* Facts
* First Ladies
* Historical Association
* India's Quiz
* Presidential Libraries
* Presidents

West Wing connections

Policies in Focus
* Overview
* Education
* Tax Relief

Theodore Roosevelt

With the assassination of President McKinley, Theodore Roosevelt, not quite 43, became the youngest President in the Nation's history. He brought new excitement and power to the Presidency, as he vigorously led Congress and the American public toward progressive reforms and a strong foreign policy.

He took the view that the President as a "steward of the people" should take whatever action necessary for the public good unless expressly forbidden by law or the Constitution." I did not usurp power," he wrote, "but I did greatly broaden the use of executive power."

Roosevelt's youth differed sharply from that of the log cabin Presidents. He was born in New York City in 1858 into a wealthy family, but he too struggled--against ill health--and in his triumph became an advocate of the strenuous life.

Twenty-Sixth President
1901-1909
Married to Edith Kermit Carow Roosevelt

Internet

▲ Roosevelt's tenure as vice president was a short one—it lasted a mere six months. After President William McKinley's assassination, Theodore Roosevelt, only forty-two years old, became the twenty-sixth president of the United States. He took the oath of office on September 14, 1901, in Buffalo, New York.

president. (John F. Kennedy was the youngest ever elected.) From the start, Roosevelt did all he could to make the presidency more powerful. He later defended his actions by saying, "I acted for the common well being of all our people . . . in whatever manner was necessary, unless prevented by direct constitutional or legislative prohibition."[1] His critics complained that he did not always let those prohibitions stop him either.

▶ Busting Up Big Business

One of Roosevelt's first actions as president was to have his attorney general file a lawsuit against the Northern Securities Company. This company had a monopoly on railroad lines in the northwestern part of the country. Small businesses and the public had to pay high rates to ship goods on Northern Security's rail lines while big companies were given big discounts.

It was risky for Roosevelt to anger the country's industrial leaders since they contributed heavily to the Republican Party. Yet, even while the conservative business community was still in shock over the Northern Securities lawsuit, Roosevelt took on the powerful coal-mining industry. Coal miners worked long hours under dangerous conditions for very little money. In the mid-1800s the first nationwide labor unions had been formed to improve working and living conditions for workers in many industries. The union formed to help coal miners was the United Mine Workers of America (UMW). Now, in 1902, the UMW declared a strike, demanding better wages and more safety measures. The strike caused a shortage of coal, which in the early 1900s was the nation's main source of fuel. Roosevelt supported the UMW proposal for an independent commission to settle the

dispute. At first the mine owners angrily rejected the idea. When Roosevelt threatened to have the army seize the mines, the mine owners agreed to work with the union to resolve their differences. In the end, the miners did not win all their demands, but they got a 10-percent raise. Most important, for the first time a president had acknowledged the equal standing of a labor union in a dispute with company owners.

In 1903, Roosevelt built on his victory against Northern Securities. He got a bill through Congress that enabled the federal government to regulate the prices that all railroad companies charged their customers. And in 1906 he got Congress to regulate the meatpacking industry after he learned of all the horrible things that went into sausages and canned meats. Upton Sinclair's novel *The Jungle* had helped to focus public attention on the unsanitary practices in that industry.

Roosevelt insisted that he was not attacking big business. He was, after all, a Republican. He realized that in the new century that was dawning, big companies were needed to run big industries like steel and oil and the railroads. But he hated the way

This photograph captures Theodore Roosevelt in 1904, the year he was elected president. Roosevelt had succeeded to the presidency three years earlier, following McKinley's assassination, in 1901.

those companies often exploited their workers and the public. He was determined to force big business to treat employees and consumers fairly, to give them what he called a "square deal." Otherwise, the bitter conflict between labor and management might lead to a breakdown of law and order in American society.

Roosevelt believed that a strong federal government and especially a strong presidency were needed to regulate big business. His attitude made many Republicans regard him as a traitor to his party and his social class. However, most

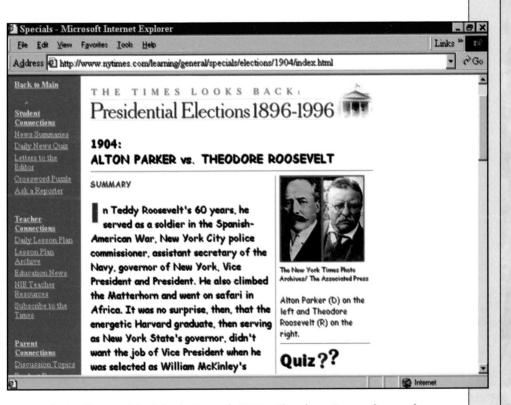

Specials - Microsoft Internet Explorer

File   Edit   View   Favorites   Tools   Help   Links »

Address http://www.nytimes.com/learning/general/specials/elections/1904/index.html   Go

Back to Main

Student Connections
News Summaries
Daily News Quiz
Letters to the Editor
Crossword Puzzle
Ask a Reporter

Teacher Connections
Daily Lesson Plan
Lesson Plan Archive
Education News
NIE Teacher Resources
Subscribe to the Times

Parent Connections
Discussion Topics

THE TIMES LOOKS BACK:
Presidential Elections 1896-1996

1904:
ALTON PARKER vs. THEODORE ROOSEVELT

SUMMARY

I n Teddy Roosevelt's 60 years, he served as a soldier in the Spanish-American War, New York City police commissioner, assistant secretary of the Navy, governor of New York, Vice President and President. He also climbed the Matterhorn and went on safari in Africa. It was no surprise, then, that the energetic Harvard graduate, then serving as New York State's governor, didn't want the job of Vice President when he was selected as William McKinley's

The New York Times Photo Archives/ The Associated Press

Alton Parker (D) on the left and Theodore Roosevelt (R) on the right.

Quiz??

Internet

In the presidential election of 1904, Theodore Roosevelt ran for president in his own right, and won by a large majority. The American people supported his progressive policies and his determination to give American workers a "square deal," which put him at odds with big business and some of the leaders of the Republican Party.

Americans supported his policies. In 1904, when he ran for president in his own right, he won by a large majority.

▶ The Venezuela Affair

Roosevelt liked power and knew how to use it. This was never more true than in foreign affairs. In 1902, Germany decided to blockade the ports of Venezuela, in South America, because Venezuela had failed to repay loans it

▲ During his terms in office, Theodore Roosevelt greatly strengthened the power of the executive branch of government. Whether in his dealings with foreign countries or with the captains of American industry, Roosevelt believed that it was the duty and right of the president to take whatever action was necessary—as long as it was not forbidden by law— to achieve the common good of the American people. His critics countered that even that did not always stop T.R.

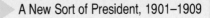
owed Germany. Roosevelt hated the way Venezuela was governed, and he despised its dictator, Cipriano Castro. But Roosevelt also distrusted Germany's intentions, and he was determined to enforce the Monroe Doctrine. That doctrine held that the United States had the right to prevent European powers from interfering in the affairs of the countries of the Western Hemisphere.

Roosevelt ordered the American fleet to move into the Caribbean and to prepare for action. Germany got the message. It agreed to submit its dispute with Venezuela to an international court to be settled. Roosevelt's tactics had been successful. His actions were an example of his motto "Speak softly and carry a big stick," which is a West African proverb that he believed in. In other words, Roosevelt used the threat of force to prevent conflicts from becoming violent.

The Panama Canal

Roosevelt was also determined to build a canal through Central America that would allow the U.S. fleet to move between the Atlantic and Pacific Oceans more quickly. An earlier treaty with Great Britain had granted the United States the right to construct such a canal. Panama, then a province of Colombia, was considered the best site for it. In 1903, Roosevelt had his secretary of state, John Hay, negotiate a treaty with Colombia, but Colombia would not agree to its terms. Later that year, however, Panama revolted against Colombia and declared its independence. Roosevelt had the United States quickly recognize the former province as an independent nation. And so it was through this new little country that construction of the Panama Canal, one of the greatest engineering feats of the age, was begun during Roosevelt's

presidency. It was completed in 1914 and opened to ship traffic in 1920.

Setting a Precedent

Roosevelt did not have any respect for the corrupt "republic" that had been created in Cuba after the Spanish-American War, either. When it looked as if civil war was about to break out on the island, he sent in the Marines to reestablish order. He acted without any legal authority, and it was not the first or last time he did so. He set a precedent that American presidents have followed ever since—sending U.S. troops abroad without first consulting Congress.

Roosevelt argued that the United States could only assert itself as a world power if it had a strong military. He did everything he could to build up the nation's armed forces, especially the navy.

Nobel Peace Prize

In the last years of his presidency, Theodore Roosevelt was especially worried about Japan. Japan had become the great power in the Far East. In 1904, Japan and Russia went to war over control of Korea and Manchuria. In 1905, Roosevelt had helped the two countries settle their differences and end the conflict. For that achievement, he was awarded the 1906 Nobel Peace Prize. Roosevelt was the first American to win that award. But Japan had demanded compensation from Russia as part of the agreement, and Roosevelt opposed those demands. As a result, the Japanese and Japanese Americans were angry with him. Relations between the United States and Japan grew worse when it became known that Japanese immigrants living on the West Coast were being treated harshly. For example, in

As president, Theodore Roosevelt built up the nation's military, especially the navy. He believed that the United States could continue as a world power only if it operated from strength.

San Francisco, California, in 1906, children of Japanese descent were segregated from other children in schools. Roosevelt did what he could to stop the racial discrimination, even per-suading the school board to end the segregation, but he was not completely successful. Many people feared a war with Japan was coming. Roosevelt's reaction was to send the entire U.S. fleet on a good-will world tour in 1907. It was the first time such a thing had ever been done. The unspoken purpose of the tour was to impress Japan with the naval strength of the United States. Violence was once again avoided. It was one more example of speaking softly and carrying a big stick.

The Great Conservationist

Theodore Roosevelt was the first president to fully realize that the natural resources of the United States needed to be managed wisely if they were to survive for future genera-tions to use. When he came into office, America's forests, wildlife, water, and mineral resources were being used up at an incredible rate. With the help of his chief forester,

On This Day: June 24, 1905 - Microsoft Internet Explorer

File   Edit   View   Favorites   Tools   Help

Links "

Address http://www.nytimes.com/learning/general/onthisday/harp/0624.html

Go

Teacher
Connections
Daily Lesson Plan
Lesson Plan
Archive
Education News
NIE Teacher
Resources
Subscribe to the
Times

Parent
Connections
Discussion Topics
Product Reviews
Vacation Donation
Plan
Educational
Products

On this Day in
History
Resources on the
Web

HARPER'S WEEKLY
JOURNAL OF CIVILIZATION

Vol. XLIX.   New York, Saturday, June 24, 1905   No. 152

Copyright, 1905, by Harper & Brothers. All rights reserved

LET US
HAVE
PEACE

http://www.nytimes.com/learning/general/onthisday/harp/0624_big.html   Internet

▲ *Theodore Roosevelt was awarded the 1906 Nobel Peace Prize for helping to persuade Russia and Japan to end their war, which had been fought over the control of Manchuria and Korea. He was the first American to receive that award.*

Gifford Pinchot, he established the U.S. Forest Service. The Forest Service manages the nation's forest resources on public lands. Roosevelt added nearly 150 million acres to the national forests. He also established the first national wildlife refuge, at Pelican Island, Florida, and created five national parks and eighteen national monuments. Theodore Roosevelt greatly strengthened the federal government's role in managing and protecting public lands. He did this over the protests of state and local governments and private companies. Similar protests continue to this day.

Chapter 5

A Fighter to the End, 1909–1919

In 1908, Roosevelt could have run for office again. He was eligible to seek another term because he hadn't been elected to his first term. But he had promised the American people that he would step down in 1908. He

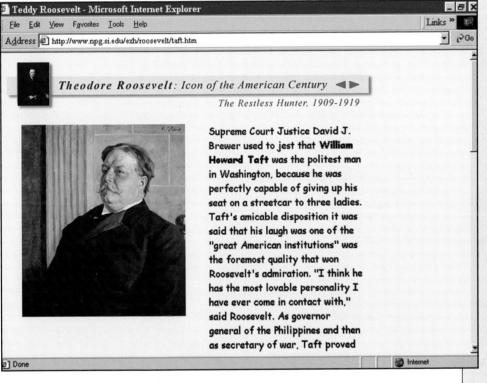

Teddy Roosevelt - Microsoft Internet Explorer

File Edit View Favorites Tools Help

Links »

Address http://www.npg.si.edu/exh/roosevelt/taft.htm   Go

Theodore Roosevelt: Icon of the American Century ◀ ▶

The Restless Hunter, 1909-1919

Supreme Court Justice David J. Brewer used to jest that **William Howard Taft** was the politest man in Washington, because he was perfectly capable of giving up his seat on a streetcar to three ladies. Taft's amicable disposition it was said that his laugh was one of the "great American institutions" was the foremost quality that won Roosevelt's admiration. "I think he has the most lovable personality I have ever come in contact with," said Roosevelt. As governor general of the Philippines and then as secretary of war, Taft proved

Done   Internet

▲ *William Howard Taft had been a trusted member of Theodore Roosevelt's cabinet and was one of T.R.'s closest friends. Roosevelt even made sure that Taft became the Republican candidate for president in 1908, and Roosevelt felt he was leaving the presidency in good hands when Taft won. But by 1912, Roosevelt aligned himself with another political party and ran against Taft.*

wanted to make sure, however, that the man who succeeded him would continue his policies. He saw to it that the Republican Party nominated William Howard Taft. Taft had served in Roosevelt's administration as secretary of war. More important, Taft had been Roosevelt's closest friend and one of his strongest supporters.

When Taft won the election, Roosevelt felt he was leaving the presidency in good hands. He spent most of 1909 and part of 1910 out of the country. First he went on a hunting safari in Africa and then on a tour of Europe. But even before he returned to the United States, he had changed his mind about Taft. Part of the problem was that Taft was too easygoing for Roosevelt's liking. Taft lacked Roosevelt's passion for reforming the Republican Party. But it is also likely that Roosevelt could not stand seeing someone else doing a job he felt he could do better.[1]

The Bull Moose Party

As the election of 1912 approached, Roosevelt competed with Taft to become the Republican candidate for president. He was supported by most Republicans, but the party machine, as usual, distrusted him. At the party's convention, they made sure that Taft was renominated. Roosevelt was furious. He quit the Republican Party and ran as the candidate of a new third party, the Progressive Party. (The Progressive Party also became known as the Bull Moose Party.) His platform was truly radical. Many conservatives believed Roosevelt actually wanted to overthrow the capitalist system.[2] Even more shocking, he declared that if people did not like the decisions of state courts, they had the right to overturn them.

A Lucky Save

While Roosevelt was campaigning in Milwaukee, Wisconsin, a would-be assassin shot him in the chest. Luckily, Roosevelt was carrying his speech and a metal eyeglass case in his vest pocket. They slowed the bullet and saved his life. Still, he was painfully wounded. In typical Roosevelt fashion, he insisted on delivering his speech before allowing doctors to treat him. It was the sort of heroic, dramatic behavior that Americans had come to expect of him.

In the three-way race for president, Roosevelt received more votes than Taft. But the Roosevelt candidacy split the Republican vote, and the Democratic candidate, Woodrow Wilson, was elected president.

Seeking Adventure

In 1914, Roosevelt's taste for adventure led him to join an expedition that planned to track the course of an unmapped river in the Amazon. His son Kermit accompanied him. It was a dangerous undertaking. Three men did not make it out of the jungle

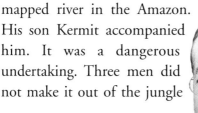
Roosevelt's dislike of President Woodrow Wilson grew as Wilson tried to keep the United States out of World War I. After the country entered the war, in 1917, the former Rough Rider became even angrier with Wilson. Wilson denied Roosevelt's request to raise a volunteer division to join the fight, as he had done in the Spanish-American War.

alive, and Roosevelt almost made a fourth. He injured his leg while trying to recover a canoe from some rapids. The leg became infected, and he nearly died after contracting a form of jungle fever. Theodore Roosevelt never fully recovered his health after that trip.

▶ World War I

That did not stop him, however, from becoming involved in politics again when he got home. Roosevelt had been angry with Taft, but he hated Wilson. When World War I broke out in Europe in 1914, with England and France fighting Germany, Wilson tried to keep the United States from being drawn into the war. Roosevelt, on the other hand, felt that America was honor-bound to enter the fight. He considered Wilson "yellow all through"[3] for holding back. In 1917, when German submarines began sinking American supply ships, Wilson was finally forced to ask Congress to declare war on Germany. Roosevelt still despised him, though, because Wilson would not allow him to raise a volunteer division as he had in the Spanish-American War. All four of Roosevelt's sons went to war, however. In 1918, Quentin, the youngest, was killed in action. Theodore Roosevelt was devastated by his son's death, though he took some comfort in the fact that his son had died a hero.

Despite his grief and poor health, Roosevelt continued to attack Wilson, criticizing him for trying to reach a peace settlement with Germany. Roosevelt felt that Quentin and the other American boys who died in World War I would have died in vain if Germany was not severely punished for starting the war. Germany was in fact punished harshly by being compelled to accept the terms of the Allies in the Treaty of Versailles, which officially ended World War I.

The treaty changed Germany's boundaries, disarmed its military, and called for reparations—payments made to the Allies for their losses in the war.

A Hero to the End

After the war, Roosevelt remained a great hero to millions of Americans. He was the favorite to win the Republican presidential nomination in 1920. But by 1918, Theodore Roosevelt was a very sick man. The leg injury and the

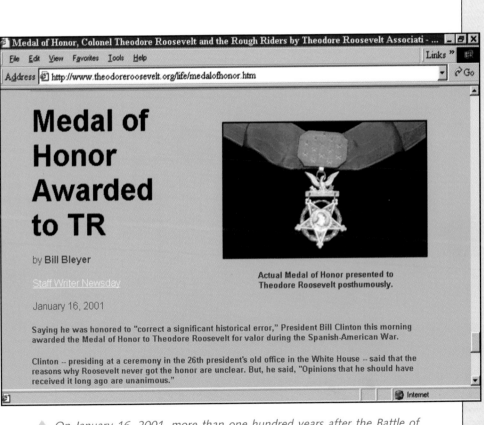

Medal of Honor, Colonel Theodore Roosevelt and the Rough Riders by Theodore Roosevelt Associati- ...

File Edit View Favorites Tools Help   Links "

Address http://www.theodoreroosevelt.org/life/medalofhonor.htm   Go

Medal of Honor Awarded to TR

by **Bill Bleyer**

Staff Writer Newsday

January 16, 2001

Actual Medal of Honor presented to Theodore Roosevelt posthumously.

Saying he was honored to "correct a significant historical error," President Bill Clinton this morning awarded the Medal of Honor to Theodore Roosevelt for valor during the Spanish-American War.

Clinton -- presiding at a ceremony in the 26th president's old office in the White House -- said that the reasons why Roosevelt never got the honor are unclear. But, he said, "Opinions that he should have received it long ago are unanimous."

Internet

▲ On January 16, 2001, more than one hundred years after the Battle of San Juan Heights, Theodore Roosevelt's bravery during the Spanish-American War was recognized when he was posthumously awarded the Congressional Medal of Honor. President Clinton, saying that he was honored to "correct a significant historical error," presented the medal to Roosevelt's great-grandson Tweed Roosevelt.

jungle fever he had acquired in the Amazon were taking their toll. After a stay in the hospital, he returned to Sagamore Hill, his beloved home on Long Island, on Christmas Eve, 1918. There, in the small hours of January 6, 1919, he died quietly in his sleep. He was sixty years old.

Tributes poured in from all over the world. Even his enemies realized that a heroic figure had passed from the national scene. As one commentator remarked, "You had to hate the Colonel a whole lot to keep from loving him."[4]

A late but lasting tribute to Theodore Roosevelt would not come until eighty-two years after his death—and more than one hundred years after the event for which he was finally honored. On January 16, 2001, Theodore Roosevelt was posthumously awarded the Congressional Medal of Honor for bravery in service during the Spanish-American War. In the citation that accompanied the medal, Lieutenant Colonel Theodore Roosevelt was honored for "conspicuous gallantry and intrepidity at the risk of his life above and beyond the call of duty"[5] while leading the charge up San Juan Hill on July 1, 1898. Theodore Roosevelt thus became the only president to receive the Medal of Honor—the nation's highest military honor—and the only person to receive that medal and the Nobel Peace Prize. Roosevelt's great-grandson Tweed Roosevelt accepted the medal from President Clinton on behalf of the Roosevelt family.

▶ Roosevelt's Legacy

Theodore Roosevelt's legacy can be spelled out in terms of specific accomplishments. His "big stick" foreign policy forced European powers and Japan to recognize the United States as a world power. The Panama Canal established an American sphere of influence in the Caribbean and helped protect U.S. interests in the Far East. At home, his crusade to preserve the nation's natural resources alone would have assured him lasting fame. He fought against the reckless overuse of natural resources by creating national parks, monuments, and wildlife refuges. He set aside millions of acres as national forests and established the U.S. Forest Service to manage those forests wisely. His social legislation—the square deal— was an early attempt to protect ordinary citizens from corrupt government and greedy monopolies. Ironically, his reforms were carried forward not by Republicans in

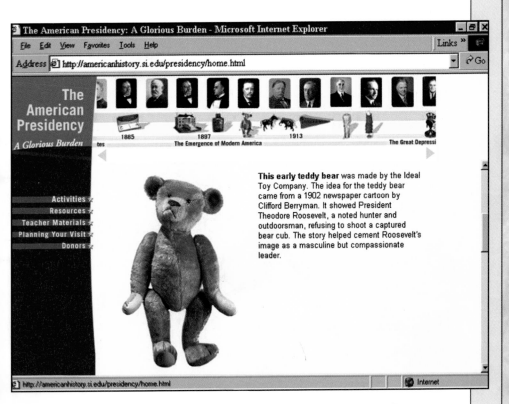

The American Presidency: A Glorious Burden - Microsoft Internet Explorer

File Edit View Favorites Tools Help

Links »

Address http://americanhistory.si.edu/presidency/home.html

Go

The American Presidency
A Glorious Burden

1885

1897
The Emergence of Modern America

1913

The Great Depressi

Activities
Resources
Teacher Materials
Planning Your Visit
Donors

This early teddy bear was made by the Ideal Toy Company. The idea for the teddy bear came from a 1902 newspaper cartoon by Clifford Berryman. It showed President Theodore Roosevelt, a noted hunter and outdoorsman, refusing to shoot a captured bear cub. The story helped cement Roosevelt's image as a masculine but compassionate leader.

http://americanhistory.si.edu/presidency/home.html

Internet

▲ The story of Teddy Roosevelt refusing to shoot a bear during a hunt in 1902 grew into legend, helped along by a newspaper cartoon—and led a toy manufacturer to market stuffed toy bears as "teddy bears."

the 1920s, but by his distant cousin, President Franklin D. Roosevelt, a Democrat, in the 1930s.

To the world's children, Roosevelt left a different kind of legacy. While hunting in Mississippi in 1902, he refused to shoot an old, injured bear for sport. The story was reported in national newspapers, and a cartoon capturing the incident became famous. As the story was told over and over, the old bear was changed into a cute cub. An enterprising manufacturer made the most of the incident by marketing a stuffed toy bear named the "teddy bear."

More than any of his accomplishments, however, it was Theodore Roosevelt's strength of character that he is best remembered for. Often described as the first modern president, he left the presidency and the federal government stronger than they had been at any time since Abraham Lincoln was in office. And he did this by giving the American people an example of courage, blunt honesty, and strong leadership that they could admire and believe in.

Chapter Notes

Chapter 1. The Great Day

1. H. W. Brands, *T.R., The Last Romantic* (New York: Basic Books, 1997), p. 354.

2. Ibid., p. 357.

Chapter 2. Weakness Into Strength, 1858–1880

1. H. W. Brands, *T.R., The Last Romantic* (New York: Basic Books, 1997), pp. 17–18.

2. Ibid., p. 19.

3. William Henry Harbaugh, *Power and Responsibility: The Life and Times of Theodore Roosevelt* (New York: Farrar, Straus and Cudahy, 1961), p. 6.

4. Theodore Roosevelt, *An Autobiography* (New York: The Macmillan Company, 1916), pp. 52–53.

5. Ibid., pp. 18, 23.

6. Ibid., p. 7.

7. Brands, p. 101.

Chapter 3. Getting Ahead, 1880–1901

1. H. W. Brands, *T.R., The Last Romantic* (New York: Basic Books, 1997), p. 163.

2. Ibid., p. 187.

3. David H. Burton, *Theodore Roosevelt, American Politician: An Assessment* (Cranbury, N.J.: Associated University Presses, 1999), pp. 49–50.

Chapter 4. A New Sort of President, 1901–1909

1. H. W. Brands, *T.R., The Last Romantic* (New York: Basic Books, 1997), pp. 420–421.

Chapter 5. A Fighter to the End, 1909–1919

1. David H. Burton, *Theodore Roosevelt, American Politician: An Assessment* (Cranbury, N.J.: Associated University Presses, 1999), p. 114.

2. H. W. Brands, *T.R., The Last Romantic* (New York: Basic Books, 1997), p. 717.

3. Ibid., p. 776.

4. William Henry Harbaugh, *Power and Responsibility: The Life and Times of Theodore Roosevelt* (New York: Farrar, Straus and Cudahy, 1961), p. 520.

5. "Medal of Honor." Text from citation accompanying the Congressional Medal of Honor awarded to Theodore Roosevelt, January 16, 2001. *The Theodore Roosevelt Association*, n.d., <http://www.theodoreroosevelt.org/life/medalofhonor.htm> (December 10, 2001).

Further Reading

Brands, H. W. *T.R., The Last Romantic.* New York: Basic Books, 1997.

Burton, David H. *Theodore Roosevelt, American Politician: An Assessment.* Cranbury, N.J.: Associated University Presses, 1999.

Cutbright, Paul Russell. *Theodore Roosevelt: The Making of a Conservationist.* Urbana: University of Illinois Press, 1985.

Gould, Lewis L. *The Presidency of Theodore Roosevelt.* Lawrence: University Press of Kansas, 1991.

Kent, Zachary. *Theodore Roosevelt.* Danbury, Conn.: Children's Press, 1988.

McCullough, David. *Mornings on Horseback.* New York: Simon & Schuster, 1981.

Miller, Nathan. *Theodore Roosevelt: A Life.* New York: William Morrow, 1992.

Morris, Edmund. *Theodore Rex.* New York: Random House, 2001.

Morris, Edmund. *The Rise of Theodore Roosevelt.* New York: Modern Library, 2001.

Morris, Sylvia Jukes. *Edith Kermit Roosevelt: Portrait of a First Lady.* New York: Modern Library, 2001.

Roosevelt, Theodore. *An Autobiography.* New York: The Macmillan Company, 1916.

Schuman, Michael A. *Theodore Roosevelt.* Springfield, N.J.: Enslow Publishers, 1997.

Welsbacher, Anne. *Theodore Roosevelt.* Minneapolis, Minn.: ABDO Publishing Company, 1998.